STOPPING LEASH REACTIVITY

A BALANCED APPROACH TO STOPPING LEASH REACTIVITY ONCE AND FOR ALL

TED EFTHYMIADIS

Stopping Leash Reactivity

<u>A balanced approach to stopping leash reactivity once and for all</u>

Published by Ted Efthymiadis
Halifax NS Canada
www.mangodogs.com

Copyright © 2020 by Ted Efthymiadis.
All rights reserved.

Cover Photo by Melissa Walker. Thanks A million!

INTRODUCTION

I knew absolutely nothing about dogs the day I adopted Phoenix from a local shelter, but, to my credit, I was committed for the long haul. In the house, Phoenix was the embodiment of the perfect dog, but when we went outside all bets were off. My back pain started the moment I opened the front door; it was like watching a team of huskies pulling a sled. Given that you're reading this book, you can likely sympathize with my issues.

After a few weeks of enduring his aggravating leash behaviours, I decided that enough was enough, and I called the shelter looking for help. They promptly referred me to a local dog trainer with more than thirty years of experience who directed me to an eight-week obedience class that was held in a church auditorium. These classes didn't help his leash issues at all. Our trainers barely spent fifteen minutes on leash walking, and the food-based techniques they taught me did not prove fruitful in the real world. After an additional two months of practicing several techniques they taught me on my own, nothing had changed and I was beginning to lose my patience. I detested walking Phoenix because he was out of control and I felt helpless.

Because we were taught that using any dog training tool that was even remotely negative was wrong and abusive, I decided to start with the more positive tools. Saying that he loathed wearing a head halter is an understatement, and he continued to pull. He loved it when I introduced a harness because it gave him more ability to pull and lunge.

We were taught two methods that now seem laughable to me but I gave them their due time and effort. I still hear other trainers recommend these two techniques every day and it's likely that you've also tried them:

- Use cut-up pieces of hot dogs to lure your dog's nose to be at your side which will prevent pulling
- The moment your dog starts to pull, stop and don't move forward until he allows the leash to be loose

While these methods might work with some dogs, they didn't work for my lunatic. After another three months, I just couldn't deal with the back pain anymore. I had been working on his leash issues for about seven months, and I was not making any progress. Phoenix was sixty-five pounds of pure muscle, and he knew that there were no consequences for his disobedience. So I finally decided to ignore the advice that the trainers had given me and I bought a choke chain.

Despite the choke chain, he continued to pull but things were even worse because he was now also hacking and coughing because he was straining so hard on the choke chain.

A few days later, I found myself at rock bottom. I had stopped on a sidewalk to give my aching back a break and was crying. Not my finest moment, but it needed to happen. I just couldn't do it anymore. This was almost 20 years ago, and I'll never forget how hopeless I felt. My pain paved the way to a new life that day, and it's the reason I'm a professional dog trainer today. That pain has inspired me to help those who feel hopeless like I once did.

Back in those pre-YouTube days, dog training information was incredibly hard to come by, but I managed to find some information about a dog training tool called a prong collar on an early police dog training internet forum. Many of the police dog trainers talked about prong collars, so it piqued my interest. When I saw a photo of a prong collar (also known as a pinch collar), I was very put off. Admittedly I thought that the prongs would stick into my dog's neck and make him bleed. The police dog trainers on this forum were incredibly generous with their time, and I quickly became friends with several of them. They all assured me that they used prong collars every day on their police dogs and found them to be a game-changer. They insisted that the collar would not make my dog's neck bleed or otherwise injure my dog and suggested I buy one as soon as possible.

The pet store I went to didn't have any prong collars in stock when I examined the collar isle. I asked the women at the cash register if she had any prong collars in stock, and she lowered her voice and whispered when she asked, "what size did you want?" I replied that a medium should work, and she looked around the store like she was making a drug deal. She bent down and rummaged under the front desk, found a medium-sized prong collar and rolled it up in a plastic bag before handing it to me over the counter. On the way home I pondered over the level of secrecy I had just witnessed, and it made me second guess my purchase. Nonetheless, I was committed to at least give it a try and so I went home and re-read my rudimentary instructions from the police dog handlers before trying out the prong collar.

Straight away I put the prong collar on Phoenix and did some basic foundation training before leaving my house. In just seconds, I noticed that he seemed much more sensitive to the prong collar than any other tool I had tinkered with previously. We went outside, and after five minutes of walking, I was crying again. These tears were not tears of sadness but tears of joy. Phoenix was practically a different dog after five minutes of training. My tears of joy were shed just two blocks from the sidewalk location that had witnessed my rock bottom tear-fest just weeks prior. That walk lasted over an hour and a half, and it changed my life. Before that day, I used to walk Phoenix for the shortest amount of time possible because it was so embarrassing and uncomfortable, and here I was finally enjoying a walk with Phoenix.

So this begs the question, will transitioning to a tool like a prong collar fix all of your leash issues with your dog in five minutes as it did for me? It's possible, but it will likely take a little more time and technique. Clearly, it wasn't because of my excellent technique that he did as well as he did. I was a dufus; the collar did the work. Having trained over a thousand dogs to walk nicely on a prong collar, the prong collar typically fixes about 75% of the issues on the first walk. My clients are always astounded by the changes they see.

If you're reading this book, you own a dog that's a hassle to walk, and I can definitely sympathize with that. I started out just like you, and now I'm a professional dog trainer who travels around the world teaching dog owners and dog trainers how to live a more fulfilling life with their dogs. People turn to me when they're convinced they have tried everything. This short book will walk you through the basic things you'll need to know to get your dog to stop pulling and stop your dogs lunging and barking when you go for a walk.

BASIC DOG TRAINING THEORY

*I*n a day and age to which many dog trainers are starting to refer to themselves as science-based dog trainers, it's convenient that we all are forgetting a lot of the science. The work of Pavlov, and B. F. Skinner have been the most Holy of Holy without a doubt. Their extensive study of classical conditioning and operant conditioning has been the gold standard for those fascinated by human and animal behavior for decades and for good reason.

UNFORTUNATELY, the findings of these great bodies of work have been cherry-picked in the dog training world. Take B. F. Skinner and his work with operant conditioning in which he outlined the difference between what's referred to as the four quadrants. Positive reinforcement, negative reinforcement, negative punishment, positive punishment. I would submit that dog trainers are known to take only what they want from the work (myself included I'm sure) to convince themselves and their clients of something they believe to be true.

IN 2015, the term science-based dog trainer started to become commonplace for trainers who used to refer to themselves as positive-only trainers, or force-free trainers. Why the shift to new a new avatar? Could it be an effort to virtue signal to the entire world how their training methods are more scientific than the methods utilized by another dog trainer who uses both positive and negative consequences? Given the extensive body of work by Skinner in particular on the realities of both positive and negative, how can anyone refer to themselves as scientific if they use a portion of the science and disregard the inconvenient part of the science?

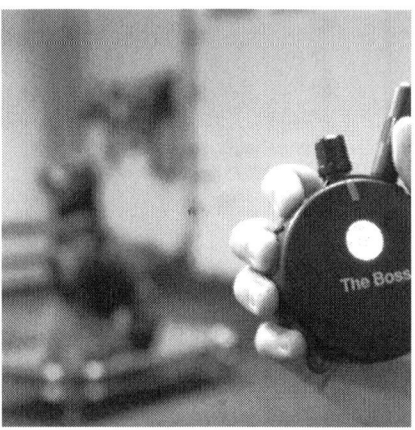

ONE OF THE most recent studies on the use of electric collars on dogs was done in the U.K by the Department for Environment Food & Rural Affairs. Around the world, science-based dog trainers were overjoyed by a study I can only imagine few of them had even read. Podcasts and blog were aflame with sensational headlines suggesting that electric collars were finally proven to be inhumane, and archaic. Clearly, I can't adequately summarize the study for you in a sentence or two, when asked for a summary of the study, Douglas Potter from Defra had this to say about the study.

. . .

"While the research shows no evidence that e-collars cause long-term harm to dog welfare when used appropriately, Defra wants to ensure electric dog collars are used properly and manufactured to a high standard.

We will work with the Electronic Collar Manufacturers Association to draw up guidance for dog owners and trainers advising how to use e-collars properly and to develop a manufacturers' charter to make sure any e-collars on sale are made to high standards.

A ban on e-collars could not be justified because the research provided no evidence that e-collars pose a significant risk to dog welfare. For a ban to be introduced there would have to be evidence showing they were harmful to the long-term welfare of dogs".

You can find a copy of the study at the link below. www.mangodogs.com/defra

If you are reading this book, you likely own a reactive dog, and it's also very likely that you've already tried a positive only flavour of training. I don't ever want to suggest that this methodology does not ever work because, in fact, it works for millions of dogs around the world each year, but I do want to underline some of its limitations.

There are really only two types of dog trainers. Dog trainers that insist they only use positive methods, and trainers who use both positive methods and negative ones.

Positive strengths:
    1. Positive methods are easy and fun for anyone to implement.

2. Positive methods keep the dog being trained happy and engaged.

3. Positive methods will increase the likelihood and speed that your dog will comply with your command.

Positive only weaknesses:

1. Positive based methods do not help create humility in the dogs that need it.

2. Positive based methods are unreliable when the distraction is very high.

3. The majority of our clients do not want to have to carry around treats for the rest of their dog's life.

Negative strengths:

1. Corrective techniques are incredible when looking to STOP bad behaviors

2. An essential part of getting to the root of things, every dog should understand that no means no and come means come. Jumping on people, pulling on the leash, leash reactivity, attacking other dogs or people.

Negative weaknesses:

1. If corrective techniques are improperly used by an owner or trainer, the dog can lose confidence in the training process. Take your time and do it right, no shortcuts.

If it's not already abundantly clear, my personal training style is one of balance. It's common for me to tell my clients "Use the positive whenever you can, and use the negative wherever you have to."

HOW YOUR DOG'S BREED AFFECTS THEIR BEHAVIOUR

*E*ach day as I work with reactive and aggressive dogs, I see the direct link between dog breeds and specific issues. If reactivity and aggression were formed by nurture alone then we dog trainers would not be seeing so many of the same issues in breed groupings. It's my opinion that many of the traits that were originally bred into these dogs' breeds are now causing them to develop serious behavioral issues.

IN YEARS GONE BY, dogs always had a job; Protection, pulling, herding and hunting were the reasons why dogs woke in the morning. In recent times, not so much. Remember this; <u>Dog's are entrepreneurs, and if you don't give them a job, they will start a business that you will hate. In many cases, that business is the business of leash pulling and leash reactivity.</u>

HERE IS a shortlist of things that I've noticed after working with thousands of dogs with leash reactivity. This will not be a comprehensive look at breeds, it will, however, be a window into the breeds that I see the most.

German Shepherds

The most common of all the leash reactive dogs, many German Shepherds are genetically hard-wired to be leash reactive. Let's briefly look at the traits that the breed used over the years to create their idea of the perfect dog. In the earliest days, they were an all-around good farm dog. In war times, they were harnessed for more extreme purposes. The all-around dog became more of a specialist, and with specialist genetics, you tend to get extremes. Defensiveness, easily startled, watchful, loads of prey drive where all things that they cultivated.

As the years have matured from the first and second world wars, the genetics were subdued when they exchanged working ability for looks. Whenever you choose looks over health and temperament, you will lose that battle. Dogs with hip dysplasia became the norm as breeds bred more and more for a sloped back. As Shakira once said "Those hips don't lie".

In an effort to resurrect the breed, many breeders have started breeding old German genetics. These genetics are typically healthy with limited hip issues, but many of these dogs are far too much animal for the average dog owner. The same genetics are being bred for police dogs and pet dog's homes all in the same litter.

Many German Shepherds are very visually stimulated. Ladies, if you have a male spouse, you know what I'm talking about. German Shepherds fixate very easily and that fixation is caused by prey drive. With prey drive comes dopamine and a higher pain threshold. (More on dopamine and prey drive later in this book) They are hard to handle because they are strong and determined, and the smallest thing can set them off. Their history as a watchful breed does not make it easy for most dog owners these days, as it leads to a lot of chaos when going out for a walk.

ONE THING that is only seen in German Shepherds is what I call the German Death Scream. The German Death Scream is the sound that most German Shepherds make when they are on a walk with two owners, and one owner walks ahead of the dog. The scream is piercing, hence the name. If you have a German Shepherd who pulls on the leash or is leash reactive, now you know why. Not to worry, it's all fixable.

BORDER COLLIES and most other herding breeds

Herding dogs without a job are always a huge pain in the neck to live with. Let's take a look at why some Border Collies develop leash reactivity. I've always had a keen fascination with Border Collies and particularly the Australian Kelpie and I was lucky enough to spend time at a Kelpie breeding ranch in Australia in 2018. These dogs are designed for one thing and one thing only, herding. It's a wonder that any of these dogs can make it through one day in the city without completely self-destructing. When given a full-time working job, they are fabulous dogs who will work all day and then sleep all night. When they don't have such a lifestyle, they often have to subsist off of 2-3 short daily walks and 30 minutes of playing fetch in the backyard.

BRED FOR INTENSITY, yet most owners don't use any of that intensity. The major trait that makes herding dogs hard to fit into normal North American homes is its physical stamina. They are designed to go all day, every day. As mentioned earlier in this chapter, a bored dog will start their own business, and sometimes herding dogs will start to pull, bark, and lunge in an effort to expend their energy. In addition to these behaviours, they are also known to redirect on the leash. Redirection is the simple act of frustration boiling up until the dog explodes and bites the thing closest to them which is frequently the owner's right leg or another sibling dog they might be walking with.

MANY HERDING DOGS do not show the classic body language signs associated with leash reactivity. Instead, it's most common to see a lowering of the head and body as they approach another dog. This being a common herding stance that has been carried over for hundreds of years in their genetics.

HERDING dogs that struggle with leash reactivity do not tend to be very vocal; they explode before most owners can notice that their dog is building frustration.

GOLDEN / *Labradoodles*

Goldendoodles as you are probably already aware, are a combination of a Golden Retriever and Poodle, and a Labradoodle is a Labrador Retriever bred to a Poodle. From what I have seen, both of these dogs struggle with brattiness while on the leash. Many of the ones that I see for training are very large, and they use their weight to get what they want. They are hard-charging when they are on a leash and that's the first thing that I work on.

I FIND many of the doodles I work with have deep barks and are very demanding. This I believe comes from the poodle genetics, as poodles can be very demanding and arrogant. They are easy to read as they have ears, tails, and tend to whine and bark a lot. They are easy to train, and this book will help you get control if you have one!

HIGH STRUNG TERRIER *Types*

I'm talking about Pitts and mixes, staffies and mixes, anything pit or staffie looking that is really high strung. I know I'm overgeneralizing, but without writing an entire book of definitions, it's the best I can do right now. Some dogs with these genetics are very calm and well mannered. I call these dogs frumpalumps and I never have frumpalumps come in for training, I only meet them when I go for walks at the park. The frumpalumps are great dogs that rarely have behavioral issues. What I see every day is the high strung, out of control, screaming their face off terriers.

IS IT ANY WONDER? They were bred for many years with hunting in mind. With hunting comes prey drive and with prey drive comes pain threshold. These dogs do not make great decisions when they are overstimulated. Many dog trainers call this the red zone, but I call it the zone. When dogs get into the zone, their pain thresholds increase dramatically and subtle techniques are not effective.

AS MUCH AS these dogs may want to behave properly for their owners, it's not going to happen with treats and praise. The key is to stop them from entering the zone whenever possible with mild-medium corrections. (More on that later in this book) These dogs make terrible decisions when they are in this mental state. Prong collars, e-collars, transitional collars are all good options, but the tools are less important than the technique. Without a human at the controls, most dogs will still go nuts, even with a corrective collar on. I love working with these dogs because it's very rare that I have to worry about one of them trying to bite me. They tend to be incredible around humans, not so much around animals and dogs. If you have one of these dogs, they can be a challenge to train, but not to worry, I work with these dogs every day, and if I can do it, you can too.

LIVESTOCK GUARDING BREEDS

The silent intimidators. Considering that I live on the outskirts of a major city, we have a lot of Great Pyrenees and other livestock guardian breeds in my area. These are supposed to be farm dogs, but they are more and more becoming city dogs without a job. These breeds have been bred to protect property and livestock for centuries, and so it's not uncommon for them to develop aggression issues. To that point, they tend to be more than the average dog owner can handle while on a leash because of their size and predisposition to defensiveness.

THE THING that one must understand about livestock guardian dogs is that they are very different in relation to all other breeds and they are very challenging for average dog owners to read. Livestock guardians do use barking to alert intruders, but I have never seen one that growls before they bite which means they are hard to read unless you know exactly what you are looking for. For the most part, they don't look at all like they are about to have an explosion to most people until it's too late. If you have one of these dogs, you should find an expert dog trainer in your area who knows these genetics well and who can help you with your dog. If you don't have access to a good trainer in your area, have someone take a video of you walking your dog and send me a link. I'd be happy to check it out and give you some tips.

WATCH your dog's eye contact, these dogs intimidate with their eyes. They don't often growl, they are strong and hard to read.

HUSKIES / *Malamutes*

The northern breeds can be a challenge for many dog owners because they are often leash pulling machines. Bred for dozens of generations to pull sleds and equipment, these breeds love to pull, it's in their DNA. The good news is that they can all learn not to pull when on a leash walk and there's nothing to say that you can't teach them a pulling sport to give them an outlet for their desire to pull.

. . .

I TEND to give them about 8-10 feet on the leash because they do really well with a little more room on the leash. Without that extra 5 feet, they tend to pull a lot more which increases their dramatics. Huskies are especially vocal and very dramatic, and so it's important that you stay calm when you are training or walking them. These dogs also use their eyes to threaten other dogs, so don't allow them to use their eyes like bullets.

TOY BREEDS

There is no difference between training a small dog and a large dog. Often, I hear small dog owners gasp when I suggest using a collar to train their dog because their Veterinarian told them only to use a harness. That's actually something that I partially agree with, however, it's not a full story. Smaller dogs do have smaller necks which are more prone to trachea and larynx issues if they pull a lot with a collar on, however, there are options apart from the harness. Harnesses are incredibly ineffective when working with dogs that pull on the leash or are leash reactive. Headcollars can be used if the small dog has a long enough snout, and prong collars can also be used because they evenly distribute the pressure of the prongs around the dog's neck so that the tender spots are not damaged. There is only one company that makes great prong collars for small dogs, and you can buy them directly from their website. Be sure to buy the quick release collars, they make getting the collars on and off much easier. http://www.kimberlandcollars.com/

AT THE END of the day, every dog regardless of the breed is still a dog. As you now understand there are some differences in how some breeds will act, but really, the training is essentially the same for any breed. Find a corrective collar that gets you some power steering and then address the issue. When your dog is making better decisions, focus more on the food, toys, praise. Simple.

THE TOOLS YOU USE WILL MAKE A DIFFERENCE

Most dog trainers are unmovable when it comes to the tools that they use. I, however, believe that it's important to have as many options as possible when it comes to solving leash problems. Just because I'm open-minded in regards to dog training tools, that does not mean that I don't have any favourites or any go-to tools. As you read further in this book you'll quickly discover that all leashes and collars have a place in the dog training world, but some tools are more effective than others.

LEASH TRAINING SAFETY

I always have two collars on the dog that I'm working with. The first collar is known as the inactive collar, and the second is known as the active collar. Think of the first collar as a safety collar in case something goes wrong with the active collar. The active collar is the nice one and snug and the one that's helping to change the dogs behavior. Think of the inactive collar like a basketball player sitting on the bench with little hope that they are going to play unless the star player gets injured. The active collar is working, and the inactive collar is waiting. 99.9% of my clients never have to rely on the inactive collar, ever, but it's nice to know that it's there in the event of an equipment malfunction with the active collar.

ONE BEAUTIFUL SUMMER day 6 years ago, I had a local dog rescue drop off a dog for some training. He was very dog aggressive and needed a lot of work. My home is on the same property as my training facility, so I was sure to remind my wife not to let our dogs out of the house. I met the owner of the rescue organization at her car, and the dog (Red) was already wearing a martingale collar at my request. I put a prong collar on him to gain some control and made sure that both collars were connected properly to my leash. After taking Red out of the car and allowing him some time to use the bathroom we started to walk towards my facility when I heard the noise of paws coming towards us on the gravel driveway. As I turned around, I saw my dogs coming around the corner. Red surely noticed them too, and so I pulled on the leash to get him to turn and follow me and then it happened. The prong collar exploded into 100 pieces. My heart sank for a moment until I saw that he was still connected to his inactive collar. I told my dogs to run back to the house, and I took Red inside the facility. Crisis averted. If I did not have two collars on Red that day, one of my dogs would most probably have been killed that day.

. . .

IF YOUR DOG IS DANGEROUS, or you lack perfect control, you need to use two collars on your dog just to be sure. Your car has two sets of brakes. The first set stops your car 99.9% of the time, your emergency break stops your car only in the event that your main brake fails.

THERE ARE three ways to connect your leash safely to your dog.
  • By connecting your leash to both your correction collar and your backup collar
  • By connecting your leash to the correction collar then using a safety clip as shown in the photo. If you use this method be sure to attach your safety exactly like in the photo. The leash is connected to the correction collar and the safety is connected to the end of the leash which then connects to the backup collar.
  • You can also use a carabiner to connect your two collars in case of a failure

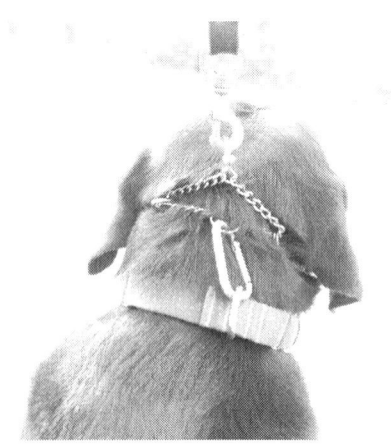

LEASHES

If I only had the ability to choose a leash or a collar, I would not hesitate to choose the collar, because the collar will move the needle a lot more than a leash. You need the most basic of leashes. A normal, straight leash of about 6 feet is perfect. Do not over think this. If you don't already have one, go to Walmart and invest $6 on a basic leash.

No bungee's, no extra loops, no bells, and certainly no whistles. If it has a compass on it, take it out to your backyard and burn it. Many dog owners desire the freedom of a retractable leash so that they can give their dogs more freedom while they are on a leash. For the average dog owner, this may be a reasonable tool, but only if the dog is not pulling them around the neighborhood or acting like a serial killer when they see another dog. Until your dog is well trained and can make good decisions on their own, do not use a retractable leash because it will make the training process a lot more difficult than it needs to be.

Harnesses

There are really two types of harnesses, top clip harnesses, and no-pull harnesses. Top clip harnesses are harnesses that allow you to clip your leash on the top of the harness between the dog's shoulder blades. These harnesses are terrible for a dog that pulls on the leash because they were actually designed to make it easier for dogs to pull. If you don't believe me, put this book down, go to youtube.com and watch 5 dog sledding videos. I rest my point. Front clip harnesses are more effective when considered next to a top clip harness because of where the leash attaches. The idea behind the front clip harness is simple. By clipping your leash to the front of the harness, you will mute the act of pulling. I've seen pulling be 95% resolved by changing to one of these harnesses, and I've also seen dogs be not phased at all by the front clip harness.

WHAT I DON'T LIKE ABOUT front clip harnesses is that they are not good for working with reactive dogs, and they could easily cause back problems with long term use, which is why some Veterinarians are against their use. Imagine that I had a harness on you when we were going for a walk and a leash connected to your chest. What would happen when you run as fast as you could forward? Your spine would twist. Many dogs have such a high pain tolerance that they don't stop pulling or lunging and this can have adverse effects on your dog's body over the long term. Feel free to try one, just stay away from the top clip option.

OFTENTIMES OWNERS of small dogs do not think that they have any option but to use a harness and that's simply not true. This maxim comes mainly from Veterinarians who tell dog owners that they should stay away from any collar, and only use a harness because their dog has a small neck and their neck / trachea / larynx could be bothered or injured if a regular collar is used. I think that this statement is accurate, but it's not entirely true. I'll make a collar suggestion later in this chapter for small dogs.

DOG TRAINING COLLARS

FLAT BUCKLE COLLARS

Flat buckle collars can be found at every pet store in North America, and if you want to do some driving around, you might even find a Harley Davidson themed collar at your local truck stop. The most common dog collar in the world, they are just a piece of webbing, plastic, or leather that is connected by a buckle. If you're like me, and most other dog owners you probably have 15 buckle collars resting in a box by your front door just screaming to be used. These collars are fine for most dogs that don't pull on the leash or lunge, but they tend to be rather useless and can be harmful to dogs that lunge on the leash. I used the word useless because they just don't do anything other than connect you to your dog. The term harmful was used because many dogs will pull when wearing such a collar, and will not stop despite their hacking and coughing. Apart from wearing one a buckle collar for fashion, I don't suggest most owners should use these collars for walking their dog.

Head Collars

Head collars are known by two different branding names, halti and head halter. They are essentially the same product with a slight variation. These collars can be very effective for dogs that pull on the leash; however, they also tend to be hated by about 65% of dogs. Over the years, I've seen many dogs that hated these collars so much that they would claw at their nose to try and get it off. As a dog trainer, I do not use these collars often because of the sheer amount of dogs that hate wearing them, but they do serve a purpose. Some dogs walk nicely when they wear them, and the tool is a God-sent for these owners. I'm not a fan of the head collar in combination with a retractable leash for obvious reasons. A dog could run 16 feet and snap their neck if they were wearing a head collar.

I ALSO DON'T LIKE these collars much for leash reactive dogs because I don't find them to be very effective. With great skill, a dog owner or trainer can use these collars to steer the dogs head up to the owner when needed (a passing dog or person). However, this technique, even when paired with treats does not seem to decrease the likelihood of dogs lunging towards other dogs over the long term. A great management tool over the short term, but not a long term solution for most dogs.

Martingale Collars

Martingales collars were originally designed for sight hounds because they have thick necks and very skinny heads which made it easy for them to slip out of traditional collars. If you are a dog owner who's had your dog slip out of a collar before, you know how terrifying. The collar will tighten when the dog or human puts pressure on the leash, and it will also release that pressure. Are they a good tool for walking your dog? Not in my opinion, but they are the best backup collar to use on your dog. Every dog owner should have their dogs wear a martingale collar every moment that their dog is outside of the home. Your leash will clip to your correction collar and also to the martingale collar.

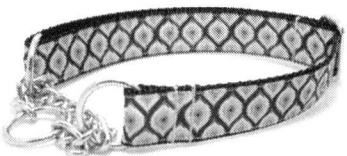

THE MARTINGALE COLLAR is used by some dog trainers as a solution for dogs that pull on the leash or have reactivity issues, but I feel that the human has to put an incredible amount of physical pressure on a dog with a martingale collar if they want to stop pulling or reacting towards things while on walks. I'm not comfortable doing that for many reasons, but the main reason is that it could hurt the dog's neck over the long term. Coupled to that, most dog owners do not have enough strength in their arms to administer a meaningful enough correction to change the dog behaviour with a martingale collar.

I ONLY USE the martingale as a safety collar. So why use the martingale for this task? Because if there is a failure of your correction collar, the backup collar will be active and if you're using a martingale there will be no possibility of your dog getting out of the martingale.

DOUBLE SAFE, just in case!

E-collar

E-collar, remote collar, shock collar, known by many names the electric training collar can be an effective tool to help you with your dog's leash pulling and leash reactivity issues. All e-collars in 2020 have several training modes and most include a tone, a vibrate, and a static pulse correction. When used properly, the e-collar can be a very humane tool, and it's by far the most versatile tool in the world of dog training. It's not my tool of choice if the client only desires on leash control, but its versatility when used for off-leash training and behavioural issues are unsurpassed. Most dog owners ask me to help them not only with leash training issues, but they also want their dog to be reliable while off leash too. It's for this reason that I do use the e-collar often with clients.

THE THING TO remember is that E-collars are usually not the easiest way to leash train your dog to walk nicely on leash and it's definitely not the most cost-effective way to get the job done. E-collars require a lot of foundation training in order for your dog to understand four basic principles. Any time you use any dog training tool to stop your dog from doing something that you don't want them to do; you'll need to teach your dog the four pillars of correction.

- WHERE THE SENSATION is coming from
  - How to turn on that stimulation (ignoring your commands)
  - How to turn off that stimulation (complying with your commands)
  - How to avoid the stimulation entirely.

PLEASE NOTE that correction must only be used when your dog is fluent in what you are asking them to do. Correction is never used in teaching a dog a command that they do not know, it's used in proofing a known command. Training your dog to understand these four principles with most other dog training collars can be done in a matter of minutes, but it takes a few weeks to do properly when using an e-collar. Foundation training takes longer with e-collar training because the e-collar stimulation is a very foreign sensation to your dog like nothing they currently understand.

Don't let me dissuade you from using an e-collar to train your dog, just know that if the goal is to fix your dog's leash issues, there are easier, cheaper ways of going about it.

Prong Collar

Likely the most hated tool in the world of dog training because of the way it looks, the prong collar is hands down the most humane dog training tool for dogs that are crazy on the leash. I know that sounds crazy but hear me out; Prong collars are a tool that does not put pressure on your dog's trachea and larynx, in layman's terms, your dog's windpipe. If your dog is wearing a normal buckle collar, choke chain, slip leash, or martingale collar, 100% of the pressure will end up directly on your dog's trachea, which clearly is not healthy over the long term.

PRONG COLLARS on the other hand (also known as pinch collars) equally distribute the pressure around the dog's neck so that their trachea is not bothered. Yes, they look like a medieval torture device, but they can be an incredible tool if used properly. If you decide to use a prong collar, make sure to purchase the right size collar and to properly fit the collar. If your prong collar is not properly fit or is the wrong size, your dog will continue to pull even with the change of collar. Most pet stores only sell two sizes and they are known as (Small to Medium = 2.25mm - Large to X large = 3mm). The collar should not be put over your dog's head like a necklace, you need to disconnect one of the links, put it on your dog's neck and then reconnect the link. If it's easy to get on, it's too big, take a link or two out. Snug is the rule, if you can get it on, it's not too tight.

A PROPERLY SIZED prong collar will give you power steering and you won't need to use much pressure for most dogs so be gentle when starting. The collar should be fit as high up on your dog's neck as possible. Don't give your dog more than a few feet on the leash when you first start with a prong collar. This is the collar that I bought at a local pet store many moons ago after struggling for a long time with my dog Phoenix and it changed his behaviour about 90% with just five minutes of training.

I'VE TRAINED about 1500 dogs with prong collars over the years and this tool will make every dog walk better in minutes. Some dogs get 50% better immediately and the other 50% can be achieved with some good leash handling skills. For other dogs like my dog Phoenix, they are 90% better in minutes. About 15% of dogs are more resistant and the collar upgrade only modifies their behaviour a small amount. Sometimes I have clients come in who have already tried a prong collar and they say that it just doesn't work when really the problem is that they are using a size that is too large, or there are 2-3 extra links in the collar which renders the collar useless. Regardless, prong collars are hands down my favorite leash training tools on the planet because they get my clients' fast results so that they can get more control and enjoy their walks once again.

YOU CAN'T HURT your dog with a prong collar. The worst discomfort that I've seen one cause is some mild skin sensitivity with a few dogs that had extreme allergies or very short hair. This can typically be remedied by buying some plastic tips to put on the end of the prongs. I don't suggest starting with the tips as they make the collar much less effective.

SLIP LEASH

If you've ever taken your dog to a Veterinarian, chances are high that the vet technician put a slip leash on your dog. It's a leash and a collar all in one. Vet's often use them because they are impossible for dogs to back out of much like the martingale collar that we discussed above. I personally don't use slip leashes with my clients for one reason only; you must have incredible leash handling skills and timing to use a slip leash. I can do it because my skill level is advanced, teaching the average dog owner to do it would take 4-6 months. It's not a great idea for dog owners try to use these leashes on their dogs that pull on the leash. The dog pulls, the client gets overwhelmed, and the dog is hacking and coughing the whole time. Slip leashes in the right hands can be a decent tool in a vet clinic, but not a tool that I would suggest using unless you are a professional handler.

Transitional Leash

Heather Beck is a dog trainer from Utah who designed the transitional leash for dogs that pull on the leash and have leash reactivity issues. She used head collars for many years before deciding to make her own product; the transitional leash. Like the slip leash, the transitional leash is a leash and a collar all in one, with an integrated safety clip just in case your dog is able to get the leash/collar off. I use these leashes from time to time, but for most dogs, I just can't justify using them. Here is the thing. Like those head collars, some dogs are fine with them and some dogs absolutely loathe them. Having trained over 1500 dogs with prong collars, I have seen maybe a hand-full who put up a fight when putting on a prong collar, yet about 65% of dogs are just miserable about putting on head collars and transitional leashes.

CLEARLY, it has to do with the fact that these dogs don't like having something over their noses which puts head collars and transitional leashes in the same boat. I do prefer transitional leashes to a head collar, however, as they are simpler to put on the dog which makes it easy to use for my clients. To be honest, I only use these leashes when I have really high prey drive dogs come in that scream when they see other dogs. The dog also needs to have a reasonably long snout or else they can easily claw the leash off their face, so it's if you've got a pug, you're out of luck. I find that they are the best thing for high prey drive German Shepherd and screaming Pitties.

HAVE a toolbox

I'm always fascinated to hear dog owners tell me that they have tried everything because that is never the case. These are just some of the tools you can try and I included them because they are the most readily available online or in pet stores. Sure, I use prong collars every day, but I always see applications for tools that I am not fully in love with. I'm not against harnesses; I just rarely see them as being effective. I don't hate e-collars; I just see cheaper, faster options to getting a dog to walk nicely on the leash. Always keep an open mind. I struggled and struggled for a long time because my dog trainer all those years ago was too closed-minded to suggest a prong collar. Do what you want to do, these are just suggestions.

OPPOSITION REFLEX

If you have a hard to control dog, it's only natural that you will want to limit their freedom while on leash walks in an effort to feel more in control. There is surely a time and a place for all dog owners with hard to handle dogs to limit movement on the leash, but this same restriction also causes more problems than it solves. When you are in close proximity to another dog, or person, you will naturally bring your dog very close to you, and that's ok because it's a move that increases control and safety at that moment. The thing to keep in mind is that if you have 10 or more feet between you and the distraction (a dog, person, and animal) it's actually better to not shorten up that leash. Shortening up on the leash should only be used if you are in close proximity to something your dog might try and bite. It keeps your dogs out of trouble and keeps others safe.

WHEN YOU SHORTEN up the leash in an effort to stop leash pulling or even lunging (when the dog is 10 feet or more away) what you are doing is activating your dog's opposition reflex. In essence, opposition reflex is a subconscious behavior that causes your dog to pull even more and lunge with more intensity when you restrain them. When humans are closely restrained in times of frustration they too tend to resist more. Remember that your dog has a different stride when they walk, they don't walk at exactly the same pace because their footsteps are roughly half of our stride. This difference in stride, coupled with the decrease in front or back movement options is not a good thing if you want to stop your dog from pulling or lunging on the leash.

RATHER THAN GIVING LESS room to move, I'll teach you later in this book how to give more room to your dog while on a leash and still get far more control and less pulling. Remind yourself that taking leash from your dog is only going to make things worse and should only be done if your dog is close enough to get themselves in serious trouble. I typically suggest the full 6 feet on the leash to be given, but many times I suggest 8-12 feet. More on that in future chapters in this book.

MANGO DOGS IS GROWING and we'll help you get up to speed on your dog training skills, handle all of your marketing and you'll be part of our team. For more information go to: www.mangodogs.com/join

TAKING BACK YOUR WALK FROM START TO FINISH

~~~

The five main reasons why dog owners are struggling with leash reactivity are;
- Reinforcing the wrong things
- Not using any correction
- Not using the right tool for correction
- Not correcting their dog soon enough
- Missing important moments

Reinforcing the wrong things
If you take anything away from this book it should be this.

<u>WHAT YOU PET is what you get.</u>

WHEN YOU PRAISE YOUR DOG, look at your dog, talk to your dog, or feed your dog, you are in essence telling your dog that you want them to show that state of mind or behaviour more frequently. I see this often with clients who are trying to soothe their anxious, reactive, or fearful dog, and I completely understand why they are doing it. It's in our nature as humans to want to soothe our dogs when they are upset. We humans seem to have a natural mothering and fathering instinct even when we are too young to be parents. I've had this instinct since I was a child and it showed up in the way that I lived with Phoenix shortly after adopting him.

ONE SUMMER WEEKEND, I took Phoenix camping and some of my friends started lighting off fireworks. At the time I knew nothing about dogs. Nothing. He started to get stressed and ran into my tent looking for shelter to avoid the noise. I ran into the tent and started to stroke him as I soothed him with my voice. "It's OK Phoenix, it's alright buddy, it's just fireworks, and they will be over soon". His level of stress at that moment was about 7/10. The next time he encountered fireworks, I did the same thing, and his level shot directly up to 9.5/10. I had no idea that what I was doing was actually making him worse. See, when I thought I was comforting him, I was actually reinforcing him. He was thinking… wait a sec; you want me to be scared and shaking? This entire principle boils down to miscommunication. I was trying to soothe but I was really reinforcing his fear.

PETTING, eye contact, praise, treats, all of these things show your dog that you want them to act a certain way, and have a certain state of time. When you give attention to an insanely excited dog, they think that you want them to be insanely excited. What you pet is what you get. So how does this pertain to leash reactivity? If your dog is reactive, do not soothe them. Don't say things like, Rover, it's ok, it's just Roxi, she's a nice dog, she lives across the street. Certainly don't pet them if they are anxious or reactive as this will only make things worse. You need to do something proactive. The great news is that you can absolutely give your dogs praise and affection, but, it should be at the right times. When are the right times? Give your dog praise, affection, eye contact, treats, etc, when they are doing the things that you want them to do and in times when they have a calm state of mind.

. . .

DON'T CODDLE at the wrong time. Snuggle and soothe when your dog is at home, being a good dog, a clam dog. Cuddle and soothe when your dog is walking nicely with a good calm state of mind. Be adamant about what you don't want. When you see your dog getting anxious, tell them what you want them to do, Heel or Walk With Me is a good option and then correct them if they do not follow your command. See the thing is, now that your dog has a bad habit, soothing will only make things worse, and giving your dog options is not likely to be effective. Then when your dog does what you ask them to do then you can go back to soothing and reinforcing.

I KNOW that this concept may seem foreign to you because it seemed totally insane to me when I learned about it, but its power should not be overlooked. Soothing my dog was not working, and I could actually see him getting worse. Praise and feed the good stuff, correct the act of not following your commands and then go directly back to reinforcing. I call this idea, positive, negative, positive. When done properly, your dog will learn to avoid any correction and will only seek the soothing fun stuff. Where are you reinforcing the wrong behaviours or states of mind? When you come home from work? When your dog is out on a walk? When your dog is at the Vet? Make a list, and develop a game plan, and do what you can to get everyone in your family to also follow the same plan if possible.

NOT USING any correction

Every dog owner in the history of the world gets a dog thinking that if they love their dog well, their dog will never develop any issues. Unfortunately, this is not always the case. I tried the exclusively positive route for a long time before I had the realization that it just wasn't going to work. I wanted it to work because I believed the words of my trainer who was adamant that I should never use any form of correction in any case with Phoenix. The thing is, some dogs are more prone to needing correction than others. Dogs who are handler sensitive are less likely to need corrections because they heed the advice of their owners when they lower their voice or show disapproval. Other dogs could not care if they piss off their owner. They want what they want when they want it. My first dog Phoenix was very independent, and not at all handler sensitive. Prey drive and dopamine desire also play a large role in the total disregard of the dog owner's commands. My dog would take off after an animal with the aim to kill it, and he didn't care how mad I would be when I got him back on the leash. To some dogs, they care more about getting what they want and less about making their owners happy. All dogs want to please their owners to some degree, but some dogs really only care if distractions are low.

THIS IS why some dogs need to learn that their owners are not asking for obedience. If you're wondering, I'm not suggesting that you yell at your dog or hit them. Start with whichever tool you desire in the list provided in this book and try them all until you find one that works for both you and your dog. Phoenix did amazingly with a prong collar and disregarded every other tool. He'd pull so hard on the leash while wearing most collars and harnesses that he would damage his throat in the process. Sometimes as dog owners, we need to stop giving options to dogs that don't make great decisions. If it were up to Phoenix, his life would consist of two things, pulling me around the neighbourhood and killing animals. Treats and praise were not going to convince him that my way was a better option than the way he wanted to live.

WHEN A PROBLEMATIC DOG does not have meaningful consequences, they learn that they can do what they want, when they want to. When you implement some proper correction with the right leash and collar, you are telling your dog that some things will not be tolerated.

. . .

I'M the kind of father who spanks his kids. The reason I don't spank my kids is that they are good kids who are very sensitive to my wife Michelle and I. When they cross a line, our disapproval is all that they need to get them to stop what they are doing. BUT, I don't assume that all kids are like this because I know some parents who have kids who would burn down their house if given the opportunity. With kids, you can give them future consequences that will help them change their behaviour at the moment. For example, Jimmy, if you don't stop hitting your sister right now, you will not get to use your iPad for two weeks. Future consequences cannot be implemented with dogs. Dogs think at the moment if something is good or bad for their current situation. Just like with kids, I don't think that all dogs need physical consequences, but it is something to think about when you have tried the more subtle methods.

NOT USING the right tool for correction

Essentially, all of the dog owners who come in for training with their reactive dogs start out with 100% positive methods. For these owners, it doesn't work as well as they had hoped, so they start to lean over to some form of punishment. Most owners dip their toes into correction by enforcing social isolation. Rover is freaking out when guests come to the home so they put Rover in a spare bedroom or dog crate. When Rover is pulling on the leash, they tell their dog that if they don't stop pulling, they will go home and the walk will be over. Both of these methods are basically useless for the majority of dogs. The owners then escalate to pointing their fingers at the dog or telling their dogs No. Again, these "punishments" prove to be useless, and then the owners tell themselves that they have tried everything. I keep detailed statistics of my clients, and over 90% of them do one thing when their dog is doing something bad and that is that they tell their dog NO and then isolate them. If No actually worked, I would be out of a job, but it doesn't for most dogs. Again, find a tool that will give you the upper hand. Corrections need to be meaningful, or else they are a waste of time. Would you send a kid to their room who loved alone time in their bedroom to read?

. . .

ALMOST EVERY DOG that I work with is terrible when guests come to the home, yet only about 10% of their owners put their dog on a leash or do anything more than tell their dog NO, when they are barking and jumping on guests. Be proactive. Find a tool that is effective; try them all, some will work better than others depending on your dog. You cannot say that you tried everything until you've at least tried all of the collars and leashes mentioned in this book. Use these tools in more scenarios than just leash walking. It's mind-blowing to me that so many people gain huge results on the leash walk but never use their corrective collar and leash inside the home to stop unwanted behaviour.

Not correcting their dog soon enough

When dog owners have tried a myriad of dog training tools and are still having leash reactivity issues, the first thing that I look at is when the client is correcting their dog. As you will read later in this book, there are many signs that the leash reactive dog will manifest before an outright explosion, with that in mind, it's likely that the dog owner is waiting too long before correcting their dog for a funky state of mind. I've had hundreds of dog owners come in with leash reactive dogs who were already using effective tools; however, it was clear to me that they were waiting far too long before administering a correction. I often tell my clients that in the first few weeks of training, they should probably correct their dog about 10 physical steps before they think that they should. What this does is reinforce how much the client is missing, and after working with thousands of reactive dogs, I have yet to meet a client that prematurely corrected their dog. We all want to give our dogs the benefit of doubt, but the problem is, your dog is not capable of making great decisions on their own yet, and thus, we should not allow them to make decisions on the leash walk yet. That part comes later.

. . .

You need to be the jealous girlfriend.

When a dating couple is walking together, the man or woman for that matter should not be checking out other people. It's just disrespectful. The jealous girlfriend does not allow her boyfriend the freedom to check out another girl who walks by in yoga pants, and you can take this way of life into your dog walks. The goal of a dog walk should not be a fixation party for your dog, it should be about the calm movement between human and dog together. Don't let your dog fixate on things that will trigger them or you will be left trying to dismantle a ticking time bomb.

Missing important moments

Sometimes my job is to help the client capture special moments that will help the dog see the walk differently. Some dog owners allow other dogs to run up to their dogs while on a walk which can be incredibly intimidating and can leave many dogs feeling that their humans will not protect them. If that's the case for you, carry an air horn and scare off unwanted dogs that get into your dog's personal space. Take control of these situations or your dog will not trust that you can keep them safe and the reactivity will continue to worsen.

Other times, clients will forget to praise their dogs in key moments when their dog has overcome a large challenge like a brief moment when a dog looks at them with a threatening stare and they do not react. If you follow the training, at some point your dog will go from being the neighbourhood psycho to walking just like a normal dog, when that happens it's very crucial to praise your dog when they don't react if other dogs bark and lunge at them from across the street. Let them know that you saw the effort that they made. Never miss a moment to make a party for your dog when it's due.

STOPPING, URINATING, POSITIONING

Every day clients ask me how much they should stop to allow their dog to use the bathroom when they go on a walk and the answer is usually that unless something is extreme, you are fine. A male dog who wants to stop every 15 steps to lift his leg on bushes, well that's extreme so it should be addressed. Your dog should give you a subtle clue that they need to use the bathroom, they should not pull you to the stop sign to use the bathroom. I don't allow my dogs to pull me ever on the leash, so they need to tell me more subtly and for them, it's usually just as simple as them looking at me. If they need to poop, that's really easy to spot.

I'M OFTEN ASKED if the dog should walk on the owner's left or right side. I don't care. Heck, I don't even care if the dog is out ahead of the client. My goal is not to develop a machine, my goal is to get the client what they ask for which is a dog who doesn't pull or freak out at other dogs, people, objects, animals. The positioning of the dog is not very critical in getting to those two goals. Any dog trainer who is reading this right now is trying not to scream and pull their hair out, and if that's you, let me tell you a quick story.

. . .

WORKING dogs were always my thing, after adopting Phoenix I got my first Belgian Malinois 14 years ago and precision was something that I spent a lot of time on. Working my dogs in drug detection and protection sports like IPO and French Ring Sport, you are scored on your dog's abilities to follow your commands exactly. My roots have always loved precision until I started to notice that my clients did not care. For many years I taught all of my clients to walk their dogs on the left side because my mentors taught me that way. I taught every client a Heel command, and when that command was given, the dog was not to walk past the owner's left foot.

ONE SUMMER DAY in 2011 I was driving to the grocery store as I noticed a big dog that I recognized who was walking with his owner on the sidewalk. As I slowed down I noticed that it was one of my clients who was walking her dog. As I watched them in my rearview mirror I noticed that the dog was way out at the end of the leash, and the client was casually walking, listening to some music and via her big red headphones.

I HONESTLY FELT A LITTLE CRUSHED. My fragile ego was not happy. These clients would come to my weekly group class every Saturday and they were star pupils, yet when I was not with them it was clear that they were not heeding my advice. I really wanted to say something the next Saturday when they came to class in a perfect heel position but I decided not to. Two weeks later I was driving to a client's house and I drove past another one of my star clients who was walking her dog. Again, out ahead, the heel was not a priority. With my ego once again crushed I really started to think about the way that I was working with my clients. One month later I drove past another star client and the same thing. That night I started a fire in my yard and resolved to stop forcing my clients to act a certain way during class if they were not acting that way the rest of the week.

. . .

8.5 YEARS later and I don't teach a heel command and I don't care what side the dog walks on. Here are the rules my clients and I agree on before we start training. Your dog can walk behind you, beside you, in front of you. Your dog can stop and pee twice per city block, but they cannot pull on the leash because it's dangerous and they are not allowed to intimidate other dogs or people when they go for a walk. My clients love how relaxed I am about things, and it's nice to see my clients not feeling the need to impress me with precision when I see them in a group class. Dog owners don't get dogs so they can train them, they get them so that they can enjoy them, and making a dog owner walk like a military exercise takes all of the fun out of having a dog.

STOP THE PULLING

*A*part from dogs whining uncontrollably, pulling on the leash is the most annoying thing in the world to me. Still to this day, I have back issues from my first dog Phoenix. He was strong and he knew it. Never for a moment did I become ok with his pulling, and I'm glad about that fact because sometimes I have clients who come in who have honestly resolved that the pulling is never going to stop. Sometimes it's my job to show the client in the first 30 minutes that it is possible just so that they can see a new way forward. Leah pulling is annoying, but it's also very dangerous for the human and the dog, and finally, it's symptomatic of a wider issue.

AS MENTIONED in the chapter about opposition reflex, pulling is a natural thing, and it can often be overcome in large part by giving the dog more room on the leash to come and go. What's not ok is when the dog is given that freedom only to abuse the privilege. If you take your dog out and normally have them on a very short amount of leash (let's say 2-3 feet) you might be able to stop 80% of the pulling by just giving them 8-12 feet of leash. Your corrective collar should cover the extra 20% if the dog starts pulling. See, here is the great thing about giving a dog more room to make decisions; it's actually the easiest way to get a dog to make better decisions if your dog is wearing a corrective collar like a prong collar. If you let a dog hit the end of a 2-foot leash while wearing a prong collar, its effectiveness will probably be short-lived. If you let them hit the end of a 10-foot leash, the effects will take hold for much longer. Using a dog's momentum against them is the name of the game, and one of the only ways I'm able to work with 100lb+ dogs without throwing out my back.

IF YOU ARE USING a head collar or transitional leash you can't give them too much leash or they could hurt their neck, 6 feet is the most that I would suggest. On a prong collar or e-collar, you can easily give 8-12 feet and not do any damage to your dog's neck. If the dog self corrects a few times and does not learn to stop pulling or lunging you can wait until they are about to hit the end of the leash and then take 2 steps back quickly. Their forward momentum coupled with your backward momentum will get your dog to check in with you a lot more. I call this a stop short correction. If an e-collar is being used, you can still use the stop short correction but you will also give your dog a correction the moment they hit the end of the leash. 8-10 feet on the leash is perfect for a stop short correction coupled with the e-collar.

DON'T LET your dog pull on the leash, it's dangerous for you. I once had a client with a big golden retriever. She did a fantastic job training her dog apart from the fact that she didn't want to use a prong collar despite my suggestion. She opted for an e-collar because she wanted to do off-leash training with him. We addressed his leash walking issues, but I could tell that the e-collar was not a great tool for her, because she was not consistent at hitting the correction button. Essentially she gave her dog the benefit of the doubt far too often. 30% of the time she would correct her dog, and 70% of the time she would let him pull her around. I told her that she was going to get hurt and that it was not fair to him because she was being inconsistent. I suggested that a prong collar would be much safer for her because it would fix her inconsistency issue because her dog would get a correction every time he pulled, and she would not even have to correct him. Unfortunately for her, she refused my suggestion. 6 months later her dog pulled her while out on a walk and she slipped on a piece of ice and she had to have an extensive shoulder surgery.

<u>Pulling is like cheating, don't sit by and watch it happen without doing something about it.</u>

SEEING YOUR DOG FROM A NEW ANGLE

Have you ever seen a photo of the side of your face before? It looks rather odd doesn't it? You can tell that the photo is of you, but it's not the way that you are used to seeing your face. Every morning you look in the mirror and see your face from the front-facing angle. You can't see your face in a mirror from the side unless you take a photo at a 90-degree angle and then look at the image which is why it's so odd to see this perspective of your own body. The same is true for walking your dog. You walk them every day and see their body walking from the same angles. When was the last time you asked someone to help you walk your dog so that you could see your dog from a new perspective. I've walked with thousands of dogs and their owners and I always want the dog's owners to walk in front of their dog, behind their dog, to the left and the right of their dog because they will notice many things that they will not notice from the angle they are used to.

Dog owners who are struggling with their dog's leash reactivity don't typically think that a new perspective will be helpful, that is until they see things from a different angle. Many times I'll have the client stand on the sidewalk as I walk past them with their dog on a leash. Then I'll have someone bring out one of my dogs, and tell the dog's owner to focus on their dog. From a stationary position, they get to see essentially every one of their dogs' angles as we walk past them and turn around. They see the earliest moment when their dog starts to fixate. They see the ears moving from a new angle and they finally notice the dog's tail for what it is; a communication masterpiece. It's hard to watch your dog's tail when you are walking them down the sidewalk, but you can see the tail in all of its glory when someone else is walking your dog.

SURELY GIVING the client a new view of their dog is important, but the reason that I like to take the leash is because the client is no longer having to do anything. You probably find yourself getting overwhelmed when walking your dog, and if you do, know that you are not alone. This is why it's so important to just watch your dog. Watch them walk, watch them freak out. Watch someone else handle your dog. Look at the ears, look at the tail, watch the eyes, something you can't see normally when walking your dog. If you want to take things one step further you could even video record someone walking your dog so that you can play it back and watch the tape multiple times. I can't stress how important it is to get a fresh view of your dog. Do not bother doing anything until you have taken this step.

MANGO DOGS IS GROWING and we'll help you get up to speed on your dog training skills, handle all of your marketing and you'll be part of our team. For more information go to: www.mangodogs.com/join

THREE REASONS WHY YOUR DOG IS REACTIVE ON THE LEASH

Dopamine

Dopamine is your enemy and you should know your enemy well so that you can conquer him in the battles that rage on your neighborhood sidewalks. Dopamine is a neurotransmitter (think of it as a hormone) that our human brains produce to increase pleasure in our brains and the same is true for a dog's brain. This chemical activates the pleasure-seeking cortex in our brains and makes us feel good, same with dogs. Ever wondered why you can't stop scrolling through your Facebook app, or Instagram? It feels good. The novelty supplies a small dose of dopamine into our ever waiting brains to satiate a never-ending itch. If you are like most people you can't help but look at your phone 100+ of times each day.

DOGS TOO HAVE THIS ITCH; however, it can be much more intense in some dogs than in humans. Some dogs seem to have very little desire for dopamine, others have a moderate desire, and others have an extreme desire. Bully breeds, boxers, herding dogs tend to suffer from extreme dopamine delivery more than most other breeds. The problem with dopamine is not only that it feels good, but it is extremely addictive. For this reason, we see dogs doing insanely damaging things to get their dopamine fix. Dogs will pull so hard on the leash that they will hack and cough, some even to the point of passing out from oxygen deprivation. Others will defy their loving owners by pulling and barking while out for a walk despite knowing that their owners are stressed by their behavior.

A DOG CAN BE TRIGGERED for dopamine production in three different ways;
- By hearing things
- By seeing things
- By smelling things

MOST DOGS ARE TRIGGERED by seeing another dog, or person or animal. Other dogs can spring to life by hearing a jingle of another dog's collar. Others erupt into a choir of barking when they see a dog on TV. Every dog's trigger will be different, but one thing is for sure, you need to stop that over-arousal ASAP.

I'M KNOWN to telling my clients that their dogs should be like a light switch; you should turn them on and turn them off. I would guess that 90% of dogs in North America turn themselves on whenever they feel like it. What's worse is that most dog owners don't have the ability to turn their dog off when needed. If your dog is a psycho when people come to your door, your dog is probably a dopamine junkie.

DOGS with extreme dopamine delivery will often have large dilated pupils when you look at their eyes during a walk. And these dogs are almost always dogs that scan the horizon from side to side when out for a walk. These dogs are not walking, they are hunting. They are looking for something to fixate on so that their brain can start producing dopamine.

. . .

So we know that dopamine makes dogs feel a state of euphoria and that it's extremely addictive but where the hell does it come from? Here is my theory. Many thousands of years ago, the ancestors of today's dogs joined forces with primitive humans. They used each other in a way to advance in a world filled with danger. The dogs used humans for food and companionship, and the humans used dogs for hunting ability, protection, and companionship. During these days, the dogs needed to help humans hunt for games if they wanted to survive, and just as a labrador retriever is more successful at hunting ducks alongside a human, so too the dogs of years gone by helped their human counterparts. I can only imagine that these dogs were robust. The weak dogs that could not perform would not have been allowed to breed. These hearty dogs would have been asked to chase wild game in less than comfortable situations.

They would need to protect themselves and others at a moment's notice, and endure excruciating pain at times when hunting for their food. The act of hunting requires few things more than pain threshold. If you've ever seen dogs hunt animals, it's stomach-churning and fascinating all at the same time. Their entire physiology changes, their pupils dilate, their pain threshold increases, their muscles bulge, they endure endless hardship, for one thing, the game. Dogs could not have survived if it were not for their ability to endure such difficult challenges, and yet when you watch a hunting dog as they endure these sacrifices, they are completely captivated by the job of hunting.

Dogs will go through incredible amounts of pain in order to hunt or chase animals, and yet we humans have decided that there is never a time or place in which using any type or negative measure in training is suitable. Prey drive is the spark that lights the fire in your dog that produces dopamine which helps your dog make terrible decisions. Your dog has all of the food he could ever want at home, yet he walks out of your front door, with his crosshairs scanning the horizon for a target. If food is not the objective, then why do they still desire such a hunt? In one word, genetics. Some dogs have been handed down genetics that still retain desires that we used to breed dogs for. Surely all of these dogs have genetics going back thousands of years, but it's key to remember that many dog breeders are still breeding dogs with these genetics in mind today. Either your dog is this way, or he is not. The genetics are what they are, they can be fostered to a small degree, but they cannot be given to a dog that does not have the inherent desire from the start.

PREY DRIVE IS the desire to hunt, it's rarely the desire to hunt, kill, and eat.

SOME DOGS NEED to hear things in order to activate the dopamine cycle, others need to see them, and some need to smell them. Watch your dogs to see what triggers them. Do they sit at the front window, waiting for hours to see something that they can bark at? Do they explode into a barking fit when hearing the slightest sound? Do they begin their escalation when another dog is way off in the distance? When you know your dog's triggers, you are better equipped to stop your dog from acting in ways that you do not desire.

REMEMBER that most dogs do not desire a fight, what they desire more is the hunt. Studies have shown that mammals actually feel more positive emotions before getting what they want than when they actually get what they wanted. This is why we spend so much time thinking about our vacation before we go on it. Why think about sex or food if it's not giving you anything in that moment? If you want to stop your dog's episodes, you need to stop them from desiring or seeking dopamine.

THIS BRINGS me to a question of ethics. If your dog is actually struggling to get a larger dosage of dopamine, then is it ethical for us humans to stop them from getting it? A little part of my soul wants to say no, but a bigger part screams yes. It's not that you are never going to allow your dog to have fun, it's that you are going to tell them when they can and how they can experience dopamine. You know that it's not ok for your dog to chase a deer across a busy highway right? We all put limits on what we will allow and not allow. Write a little note on a piece of paper that says "I am taking my dog for a walk, and he's lucky that he can come on my walk. It's not going to be about him until he proves to me that he can deal with the way that I like to walk." Tape the paper to the inside of your front door, and read that note every time you go for a walk.

Fear

In 2020, it's not uncommon for a dog trainer to teach that 100% of aggression is based on fear. While I do think that fear can be a reason why some dogs react on the leash, I don't think that fear-based reactivity is very common. Many trainers drop the F-bomb without any proof of fear and are driven only by ideology.

It's easy to assume that when a dog has any type of negative engagement with other dogs that this would cause fear right? Surely this does happen. Take the dog that is walking with their owner down the sidewalk on a leisurely stroll when a dog leaps through the screen of the front door and comes bounding at your dog. If my dog was attacked in this scenario, it's easy to assume that it was the dog accosting them that caused my dog to start acting differently. Every dog shifts into the state of mind that my best defense is a good offense. Yes, this does happen to some dogs.

Something similar can also happen when dogs are attacked while they are being walked. Some of the dogs that I work with process the attack differently, they don't treat it as a bad thing rather it's a good thing. They anticipate fighting because it's a way for them to reach the highest level of dopamine production possible in a mammal. Remember that dopamine is addictive and pleasurable. So many of these dogs that have been attacked are deemed fearful when in reality they desire the tussle.

A FEW YEARS ago I worked with a pitbull named Atlanta. She was a sweet dog with people but a freaking lunatic around other dogs. She was owned by a very nice couple who adopted her from a rescue who sent her to Canada from Georgia. Atlanta was fine with other dogs when she came to Canada for the first 6 months until she was attacked while out for a walk with her owner. Her owner understandably was convinced that Atlanta was fearful because of the attack, and so she had tried plenty of positive methods and trainers before calling me to get another opinion. After listening to the owners over the phone, I told them that it was entirely possible that Atlanta was fearful of other dogs, but that it was also possible that she was not fearful at all. I went on to tell them many stories of dogs that I had worked with like Atlanta to try and give them some context.

A WEEK later they brought her in to meet with me. She was as sweet as a Georgia Peach, but holy Moses, she was insane around other dogs. I asked them if she had ever been in a dog fight or attacked any other dogs and she had a handful of times. One time she jumped into a lake, swam across the lake and attacked a dog on the other side of the lake. After hearing the story it was not hard for me to convince them that Atlanta was not afraid, she was just doing everything that she could to get her dopamine. All of the classic signals were present, when they would take her for a walk, she would scan the horizon from side to side for dogs, ears up, tail up, escalated breathing, hair up, etc. In some ways, they were pleased to learn that Atlanta was not fearful because they could now learn how to actually address the root issue. After just 4 lessons, Atlanta could be around other dogs, walk nicely without pulling and her leash barking and lunging were things of the past. She needed a few rather intense corrections, and a lot of praise, and food, but it wasn't rocket science.

So LET'S examine some easy methods to help you understand if your dog is fearful or if your dog is desiring to act in such a way.

• FEARFUL DOGS ARE NOT LOOKING for a fight, they are only protecting themselves when everything else has not worked to secure safety
• Fearful dogs do not draw attention to themselves. They don't scream like dying animals every time they see a person or dog that they are afraid of
• Fearful dogs avoid conflict
• These dogs are almost always insecure dogs before they were attacked
• These dogs only react to other dogs or people that threaten them directly, they do not overgeneralize to ALL DOGS or ALL PEOPLE
• They do not scan the horizons looking for other dogs unless they are near a specific place where they were previously attacked

IT ALWAYS FASCINATED me that so many dogs are attacked every day by other dogs and most of them never develop any behavioural issues because of what happened. These dogs often lay on their backs when they are attacked until it's over, and they bounce back within minutes or hours of the event.

IF YOU ACTUALLY HAVE A FEARFUL dog I believe that the training approach should be different than when a dog is choosing to act like a maniac for reasons we will address later in this book. A fearful dog needs advocacy, which simply means that they need you to step up as a dog owner and not let other dogs intimidate them or get in their personal space. You'll want to buy a very loud air horn from a local boating store (many stores like Walmart also stock them) so that you can blast it at any approaching dogs with an ear exploding sound blast if they run after you and your dog when you are walking your dog.

IF YOUR DOG is fearful of people or dogs approaching, they are afraid of several things;

- THEY ARE afraid of the approaching dog or person
    - They are afraid that they are on a leash and can't getaway
    - They are afraid that you will not be able to stop the aggressive dog or person who will not leave them alone

THE FIRST TIME you blast an approaching dog in the face with an airhorn and it runs away, your dog will look up at you like you are a superhero. If you can't PHYSICALLY protect your dog, they will never trust you enough to remain calm when other dogs are nearby. If your dog is fearful of people approaching them, buy a bright orange leash on Amazon.com that says Warning or caution on it. If people approach, tell them that your dog has rabies and walk away. Some people will avoid you when they see the leash and others will not don't stick around to find out what those unbalanced people are going to do next.

IT'S RATHER simple to determine if your dog is fearful or not. Is it your avoiding conflict until there is no other option? Or are they seeking conflict? Was Atlanta avoiding conflict when she swam across the lake to attack another dog? Hardly. Does your dog ever go out of their way to seek conflict with other dogs who are avoiding them? If the answer is yes, your dog is not fearful. Some food for thought.

FRUSTRATION
Many of the dogs that I work with that are leash reactive go to

doggy daycare. It's hard to believe that a dog looks so convincingly like they are aggressive when they go to daycare five days a week, but in my world, it's an everyday thing. Think about it, 100% of doggy daycares are like all-night raves, but for dogs. They see playing with dogs as their right, not as a privilege.

MOST DAYCARE DOGS hop into the back of their owner's car at 7:30 am after being given their breakfast and enough time to use the bathroom outside. They are full of energy, and they know where they are going. The whining starts immediately, even before the car has been started. With each traffic light that they pass, their dog becomes more enthusiastic. Five minutes into the drive, it's a full-on dance party in the back seat, the dog has transformed into a canine version of Richard Simmons. As they round the final bend to the daycare facility, the barking is so piercing that the owner can't take it anymore.

AFTER CLIPPING on a leash to the dog's collar or harness, the dog pulls them to the front door without any consideration for their dog owner. The dog bounds at the gate, only to be handed over to the daycare attendant who will immediately give the dog exactly what they want. Crazy, unreserved, high arousal play. Or...more dopamine.

WHEN DOGS PLAY with such reckless abandon, many things are happening at the same time. There is social stimulation, meeting old friends once more, dominance/submissive posturing, excitement, frustration, and increased pain threshold. When dogs receive so many positive sensations under one roof, it's no wonder why they start to over-generalize their excitement into different areas of their lives. With each passing day of daycare, their bodies come to expect the 3rd highest level of arousal only surpassed by fighting, and breeding. They start to crave the dopamine that they desire, and it starts to flow the moment the dog owner puts on their shoes at the front door each morning.

. . .

It's no wonder that these dogs go crazy when their owners take them for a walk. Most of them have little to no impulse control and see other dogs like they are a piece of sporting equipment. They pull towards other dogs, whine, and bark, while the owner allows it to happen. After a few weeks of this, the owner stops allowing dog/dog greetings on walks because their dog is getting into fights when they approach other dogs. So why do these (social dogs) start getting into fights with other dogs on the sidewalk? Have you ever been walking down the street and had someone walk up to you, and push you over, then put their hands in your pockets, as they blow their coffee breath in your face? Yeah, sounds like fun to me too.

Technically these dogs are social dogs, but their social skills are so repulsive to a normal dog that their presence is rarely well-received. These doggy daycare nutjobs are just out of control. Always given what they want. High arousal outlets for their energy instead of obedience, control, discipline. These dogs require some level of correction to get them to behave properly while on leash walks, but they tend to be easy to work with when they realize that the world does not revolve around them getting whatever they want to get when they want it.

To someone who's never seen a boxing match, boxing looks like two humans doing their best to kill each other. To someone who knows even a little bit about boxing, they understand that death is not the goal. Every boxer boxes for different reasons, but killing is not the goal. Competition, excitement, money, frustration, prestige, exercise, titles, these are the goals. Remember this example as it illustrates how a human can act so aggressively without hatred or desire to kill. So too, dogs can look like they want to kill when in most cases, they are bundles of frustration looking for an outlet.

THE BODY LANGUAGE YOU'LL NEED TO NOTICE

It's my view after training thousands of dogs with leash reactivity that dog owners are usually incapable of reading their dog's body language accurately. I didn't say this from a judgmental place because I don't expect dog owners to know anything at all about dog training. As I'm known for saying "I don't expect you to know these things, your dog is a different species. Relax, I'll teach you". Reading a dog's body language is part science and part art form. The science reference is made because certain breeds will communicate via body language in ways that you can expect 100% of the time. The art reference was made to illustrate that even the pros are not perfect at reading dogs. One of the things I love best about my job is that I don't know everything there is to know about dogs, despite investing 13,000+ hours into the craft. However I am able to read dogs better than the average dog owner, so I hope to help you with that in this chapter.

REMEMBER that body language is a subconscious behavior, so your dogs can not lie to their surroundings. Humans can use their body language in ways that help them convince others that they are feeling a specific way, but these are fabricated motions that are not accurate.

When a dog's tail is doing something, the dog has not tried to move its tail in such a way as to convince anyone of anything. The movement is subconscious. Their ear, tail, muscle tension is about as natural and organic as you breathing right now. You don't try to breathe, you just breathe. This is one of the reasons why I love working with dogs, I never have to worry if I'm being lied to.

MOST REACTIVE DOGS are easy to read if you know what you are looking for.

SCANNING

About 70% of reactive dogs are scanners. By scanners, I'm referring to the way that the dog views the walk. These dogs move their heads side to side, from left to right, looking at eye level. The behavior is noticed more in bully breeds and herding dogs but can be noticed in most breeds or mixes. The scanning looks to the untrained eye like nothing at all, and most of my clients do not even notice that their dog is doing it until I mention it. Scanning is a habitual behavior that reactive dogs develop after going for dozens of walks in which they have explosions of reactivity. (Barking, growling, lunging) These dogs scan the horizon for dogs, people, animals, not because they are scared, but because they are trying to fulfill a need.

SCANNING IS the first sign most reactive dogs will show, and is typically seen the moment the dog leaves the front door and has not yet left the driveway. These dogs desire dopamine, and they are always dogs that are easily stimulated. They hear everything, they see everything, they miss nothing. Why? Because they are not on a walk, they are on a hunt. Scanning must be stopped if you are going to master your leash walks and rid your dog's life of their reactivity. An easy thing to remember is that reactive dogs should not be given a lot of freedom in the beginning until they can handle that freedom, so your dog should not be scanning the horizon. If you are doing a transitional collar or head collar, pull their head up and make them stop scanning. With a prong collar or e-collar, a stop short correction will help to get them more focused on you. The reason that so many dog owners miss the scanning is that it looks very innocent and it's silent. Let me ask you a question, if you saw a man walking down the street, scanning from side to side, chest out, head up, would you not be concerned? I've seen people walk like this downtown at night time after getting out of a bar and I avoid those people like the coronavirus. That's what your dog is doing; don't allow them to scan, because it's only going to lead to barking, growling, and lunging. Scanning is the gateway drug to an explosion.

Ears

As mentioned in the above section on scanning, most dogs will scan as their first indication that they are preparing for an explosion, but some dogs do not scan. These dogs are a lot more casual as they walk down the driveway. If your dog is not a scanner, the 1st sign that you will notice is your dog's ear flicking up.

A DOG's ears can do an incredible amount and it's a shame that so few humans know how to read a dog's ears. Back, 360, TV antenna, Up, Forward, are all positions that a dog's ears can use to indicate their mental and physical state.

Back ears

Ears back is typically a good sign when walking a dog because it denotes submission. Many dog trainers will suggest that a dog is fearful when their ears go back which is an overgeneralization. A dog puts their ears back when they are being petted by their owner, so it's not always a fearful action. Most dogs will put their ears back when their owner walks towards them. The only time that ears back is a sign of fear is when the dog's ears are back and their tail is tucked underneath their body. When your dog's ears are back if you are on a leash walk, it's a good thing. A sign of reverence, not of fear.

IF I WERE on a walk with the queen of England, I would have my ears back. I don't have to be terrified of her in order for me to change my body language to show reverence. The next time you go out for a walk with your dog, make a mental note on how much of the walk your dog's ears were up and how often they were back. If you have a leash reactive dog, chances are that your dog's ears are forward more than they are back. If you see ears back while on a leash walk you have nothing to worry about at that moment.

360 EARS

360 ears are what I like to see when walking a client's dog or even my own dogs. They are up but they are pivoted to the side. These ears suggest interest in their surroundings with a touch of humility and reverence. If you see 360 ears while on a leash walk you have nothing to worry about at that moment. 360 ears are always nice to see.

TV ANTENNA EARS

TV antenna ears are another positioning for ears that are rarely seen when a dog is walking. They are more commonly seen when a dog is doing something stationary like sitting or laying down. They are a good positioning to have just like the 360 ears, however, these ears denote softness, contentedness, and calmness. If you see TV antenna ears while on a leash walk you have nothing to worry about at that moment.

UP EARS

Arguably the most difficult position to understand, when a dog's ears are up, we believe that they are happy, excited, or enthusiastic. These words do accurately describe how a dog can feel when their ears are up, however, we must integrate context into the scenario. If you call your dog from the living room to the kitchen and say something like "Rover, come and get a treat" it's to be expected that their ears will be positioned up when they enter the room. When the reactive dog's ears are up when/while on a leash walk, their state of mind is not one filled with humility; they are in a state of anticipation and arousal. I do not like to see a reactive dog's ears fixated up for more than 3-4 seconds while on a leash walk. When your dog is looking to the horizon with ears up, even if they are not scanning, they are focused on what could be coming, and they are not in the state of mind that I would desire.

I WANT to see ears back, 360, or TV antennas because they all include humility. When the ears are up while on a leash walk, you will often see the dog's chest pushed forward which is also not a good sign of things to come. On the whole, when I'm walking with a client and their dogs, I want to see the dog's ears back, 360 or TV Antenna. If they flick up for 3-5 seconds I will allow it, but not more than 5 seconds. If I am on a walk and the dog's ears are in a good position (back, 360, TV Antenna) but quickly move to the up position when they see a distraction, they are immediately corrected for their change in their state of mind. It may seem overbearing but it's essential that you communicate with your dog in a way that tells them that you know what they are doing and that it will not be tolerated.

FORWARD

Did you know that a dog's ears can pivot forward? Most dog owners are not aware of this position because they see their dogs while only from behind, and at that angle it's difficult to spot the difference. As you'll notice in the photos, it's a subtle difference but a very important one. This slight change from up to forward is most easily seen in dogs with pointy ears like German Shepherds, Huskies, Akitas, and the like. Cropped ears are difficult to read, and floppy ears are also difficult to read if they are up or forward. Ears forward are not something that you want to see while walking your dog because the ears denote a strongly fixated mental state in a direction that we don't desire. If you watch carefully, you'll also notice this forward position in dogs that are in a predatory state. Either way, your dog should not be showing ears forward when you go for a walk for any reason at all.

TAIL

Not only useful for knocking coffee cups off of your coffee table, but a dog's tail can also give you an extensive education about how your dog is feeling while you are out for walks. Some dogs almost always carry their trail high. Huskies, Malamutes, Akitas come to mind, however, many others also exist. It can be difficult for even a dog owner to read these tails but they do have three positions. With these breeds, I do not expect the same tail position that I would expect from a German Shepherd. When on walks I look more for looseness/stiffness than I do for the position of the tail. A loose curl for these breeds is fine, and it is often accompanied by a slight bounce from side to side. What is alarming is when the tail tightly curls over the back and remains stiff. The stiffer the tail, the more danger you are in.

DOGS with more conventional tails are much easier to read. The longer the tail, the easier it is to read. With these dogs, I like to see a tail that is between the 7-10 positions on a clock if your dog is walking on your left-hand side. The 10-2 position is the danger zone. 3-6 indicate fears and the dog needs more confidence. Remember that the closer their tail is to their back, the more focused they are. You'll see that you can actually change their tail positioning when you correct them. The ears will shift back and the tail will lower slightly or loosen its stiffness. Remember that these changes in body language are subconscious and a moment by moment window into your dog's state of mind.

BREATHING

The next step in escalation is what I call loaded breathing. Loaded breathing is the dog's way of taking in more oxygen because they are preparing for an upcoming explosion. They are short breaths but deep and easy to hear. When your dog is laying next to you on the couch, you cannot hear them breathing. When your dog is walking calmly beside you, you cannot hear their breathing. When your dog has loaded breathing, you can hear it even when you are outside on a busy street. If you are still struggling to understand what loaded breathing is, get up off your chair right now and run as fast as you can for 20 seconds, then stop and listen to your breathing. Loaded breathing is rarely heard at the very beginning of the walk, typically it's heard when the dog has seen another dog off in the distance, their ears have moved forward, their tail too and then we notice the breathing. If you ever hear escalated breathing it's a bad sign. A sign that you missed a lot of things on your walk. A sign that you have almost lost your dog completely at that moment. Much can be done to bring them back, but it will have to be done quickly.

HAIR

A dog's hair will stand up on their back for a number of different reasons.
- Fear
- They are overly aroused
- Nervous energy

MANY DOG OWNERS have been led to believe that when their dog's hair stands up on their back, it must be because they are fearful. This over-generalization has been perpetuated mainly by dog trainers and it's not totally accurate. When you notice hair standing up from the back of the neck to the tip of the tail, this is a typically a fearful/defensive response. When you notice a small section over the dog's shoulders, this represents a dog that is overstimulated or overly aroused. When you notice a section over the shoulders and at the tip of the tail, this represents a nervous energy.

When a dog's hair is up while on a walk, this leads me to again believe that the dogs are far too overstimulated and fixated than he/she should be. You might have missed the scanning, missed the ears up or forward, missed the tail high and stiff, missed the escalated breathing and now the hair standing up is your last chance to avoid an explosion.

Remember that the longer you wait to correct your dog's funky state of mind, the more intensity you will have to use when you correct your dog. Every step that your dog takes towards another dog, person, or animals will increase your dog's arousal and in turn, your dog's pain threshold.

Most dogs don't need much correction to get them to stop increasing their arousal if it's done early.

Explosions

When all or most of these signs have not caused us to remedy our dog's state of mind we'll inevitably have to collect the pieces after the explosion. The scanning, ears, tails, breathing, and hair are all signs that indicate that the explosion is coming. Most dog owners do not start to do anything until they are in explosion mode. For me, it's the exact opposite. If I miss everything, I do not try to remedy the situation, I just keep walking and try to learn from the failure that I just witnessed.

. . .

WHEN YOU ARE out on a walk with your reactive dog, everything happens with such speed that it's incredibly hard to put everything together unless you know what you are looking for. This is why I give my clients only a few things to focus on when walking their dogs. I make sure that they know the signs listed above and I remind them their job is to defuse the bomb before it can go off. If you don't do it perfectly, it's ok because you can learn with each passing distraction if you are mentally equipped to know how to address the issue the next time. My clients are all reassured that I do not expect them to have a perfect dog by the time we meet for our 2nd lesson. I do this to remind my clients that the goal is not perfection, the goal is progression. Even after all of these years I still miss things, just 10 days ago I was walking with a client and three little dogs came out of a trail and started barking at my client's dog, I grabbed the leash hoping to be able to defuse the bomb but it was too late. It was not my fault, not the dog's fault, nor the client's fault, but we did learn what didn't work at that moment. Cut yourself some slack, you deserve it.

SOME LEASH REACTIVE dogs are incredibly easy for me to get to walk nicely, and honestly, some are a huge pain in the ass. Be patient with your dog during the training process and never blame them if things don't go according to the plan. Dog training is not a perfect science. It requires an open-mindedness. The best dog owners are the ones who are the most open-minded.

Ted Efthymiadis
    www.mangodogs.com (my dog training business)

ALSO BY TED EFTHYMIADIS

All titles are available on Amazon in Kindle and Physical book some, some are available in audiobook version from www.audible.com

E-Collar Training for Pet Dogs

Giving Up On My Dog: A straightforward directive for those close to giving up on their dog

Prong Collar Training for Pet Dogs: The only resource you'll need to train your pet dog with the aid of a prong collar (Dog Training for Pet Dogs) (Volume 1)

Potty Training Puppy: A comprehensive guide to help you navigate the crappy job of house training your puppy

Thriving Dog Trainers: An indispensable tool to help you start or repair your dog training business (Business books for dog trainers)

Thriving Dog Trainers Book 2: Get better clients, work less, enjoy your life and business (Business books for dog trainers)

Made in United States
Orlando, FL
21 June 2023